150

JOKES

for

Monstrously

FUNNY KIDS

Authors
Lia Leow & Aaron Tay

Illustrator
Robin Tay

PREFACE

When my son, Aaron, was undergoing treatment for lymphoma (a type of cancer), his taste buds were affected. This caused his appetite to decrease drastically.

In a bid to cheer him up, I started coming up with jokes to make meal times more fun. Soon after that, Aaron and his younger brother, Robin, started coming up with their own jokes, which were way funnier than mine!

This book is a compilation of the jokes we came up with as a family. We hope it will bring you as much joy as it did for us to write and illustrate it.

Love,
Lia Leow & the Monster Thinkery family

TABLE OF CONTENTS

BONUS FEATURES IN THIS BOOK!

You will find the following icons in this book:

These are some interesting or hilarious facts that we would love to share with you!

Why did the people stand outside in the rain for a meeting?

They were trying to brain-storm ideas!

Aaron and Robin would love to see your illustrations! Draw on a piece of paper or in the space provided. Let your creativity run wild! Ask your parents to send your drawings to us and we may just share them with our followers! Our contact details are at the end of this book.

JOKES START HERE!

1. What is the loudest part of a tree?

   Its bark!

2. Why did the art collector go to the doctor's?

   The art collector had many pain-tings!

3. Why did the parrot's owner refuse to bring it out for a walk?

   The owner did not want his parrot to turn into a walkie-talkie!

4. Which candy makes the most noise?

   The lolli-pop!

5. Which bird is a good baker?

A mag-pie!

6. What candy did the hikers find near the swamp?

The marsh-mallow!

create your own drawing!

7. What do clouds decorate presents with?

Rain-bows!

8. Which fruit has a belly button?

A navel orange!

9. Which place does the alphabet like to visit?

The post office! Because it is full of letters!

10. What is a vehicle's favourite TV programme?

A car-toon!

11. Why did the farmer avoid walking past
    the stable at night?

He did not want to have night-mares!

12. Why did the egg roll away from the farmer?

It wanted to egg-scape (escape)!

13. Why did the house go shopping at the clothing store?

It wanted to get a dress (address)!

14. What did the butcher use to drive the nail into the wall?

A ham-mer!

15. Why was the grumpy man always in pain?

Because he was a gr-ouch!

16. What is a father's favourite fruit?

The papa-ya!

We are family!

66

Did you know...

that a papaya is actually a large berry?

99

17. Tom wears glasses. Why can't he stop laughing?

He has his spec-tickles (spectacles) on!

Wahaha! I can't stop laughing!

18. Why can't the king stop measuring things?

He is a ruler!

19. Which musical instrument disagrees the most?

The pia-no!

20. Which musical instrument is the stickiest?

The gui-tar!

21. Why is the panda good at scaring others?

It eats bam-BOO all the time!

22. What is a dog's favourite number?

The number '9'. Because a dog belongs to the ca-nine family!

23. What do you say to a dog that is having a bad day?

I'm sorry you're having a ruff (rough) time!

24. Which rodent oinks?

The guinea pig!

25. Daryl played a prank on Lionel. Why did Lionel fall down?

Because Daryl pulled Lionel's leg!

26. Why shouldn't the farmer milk a cow at night?

Because milk is a day-ry (dairy) product!

27. What did the scientist say when he made a yucky discovery?

Eeew-reka (Eureka)!

28. Which bird writes well?

The pen-guin!

29. When was the clock rude?

In the mean-time!

30. Which mystical animal likes to eat corn?

The uni-corn!

31. What do you call a kangaroo that needs to go to the toilet?

A kanga-loo!

32. What do you call a walking stick that is in a rush?

A hurry-cane (hurricane)!

33. What do you get when a battery plays a prank on a light bulb?

Elec-trick-city (electricity)!

34. What do you get when you listen to a candle talk nonstop?

Ear-wax!

35. Which letter is the sleepiest?

The letter 'zzzzzzzz'!

36. Why did the lady kiss the twig?

She wanted to put on some lip-stick!

37. What do you call a horse that lives next door?

A neigh-bour!

38. What is the most fun part of a house?

The toy-let (toilet)!

39. Which insect can be used to support buildings?

The cater-pillar!

We will become butterflies soon!

40. How would you describe someone who is good at rowing a boat?

Oar-some (awesome)!

41. Why did the burglar wear black gloves?

He did not want to be caught red-handed!

42. Why is the animal lover happy whenever there is a thunderstorm?

Because it rains cats and dogs!

43. Why did the spider fall in love with the duck?

The duck has webbed feet!

44. Why do other vehicles avoid the strawberry truck?

It causes a jam wherever it goes!

45. Why was the snowman nervous?

He had cold feet!

46. Which plant is a chatterbox?

The beans-talk!

47. What bug can you use to measure things with?

An inch-worm!

48. Which letter holds the most water?

The letter 'C' ('sea')!

49. Why did the chef tell the boiled eggs a joke?

He wanted to crack them up!

50. Which vegetable comes from a chicken?

The egg-plant!

51. Which country is the most creative?

Imagi-nation!

52. What pet does a carpenter keep?

A wood-pecker!

53. What do you call a frozen burger?

An ice-burg (iceberg)!

54. Why did the farmer ask the cow to dance?

He wanted to make a milk-shake!

55. What type of bean wobbles?

A jelly-bean!

56. Which letter looks the yummiest?

The letter 'O'! Because it looks like a doughnut!

57. What has 8 legs and is good at finding out secret information?

A spy-der (spider)!

58. What happens when the sky gets dirty?

It takes a rain shower!

59. Why is the martial artist good at telling jokes?

He knows how to throw a good punch-line!

60. Why did the hiker keep dozing off?

He was carrying a nap-sack (knapsack)!

61. Why is the pirate good at painting?

He is a natural arrr-tist (artist)!

62. Which is the most terrifying part of our body?

The scare-leton (skeleton)!

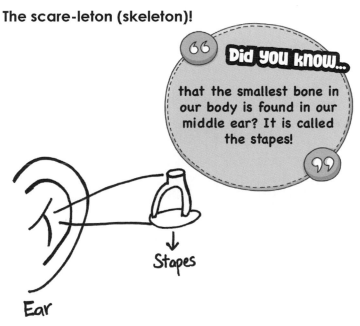

Did you know...

that the smallest bone in our body is found in our middle ear? It is called the stapes!

↓
Stapes

Ear

63. What is the cheapest electrical appliance?

A free-zer!

64. Which day do you drink the most water on?

Thirst-day (Thursday)!

65. Which reptile likes to eat pie the most?

A pie-thon (python)!

66. What pet does a knight keep?

A sword-fish!

67.   Why did the boy put stickers on his teeth?

He ran out of tooth-paste!

68.   Which fruit can you sit on?

A chair-ry (cherry)!

69.   Why is the dog so cheerful?

It is paw-sitive (positive)!

~WOOF!
GIMME
A
HIGH FIVE!

70.   What happens if all shellfish go extinct?

It will be a clam-ity (calamity)!

71. What do you say to an ear of corn when it gets a new job?

Corn-gratulations (congratulations)!

72. What is the best day to eat ice cream on?

Sunday (sundae)!

73. Why does the alien often daydream?

He always spaces out!

74. What do you call a two-wheel vehicle that keeps saying, "See you later!"?

A bye-cycle (bicycle)!

75. Which sport is the alien with ten legs good at?

Tennis! Because he has ten knees!

76. Why did Santa Claus bring along an umbrella on Christmas Eve?

Because of the rain-deer (reindeer)!

77. Why did the lamp feel dizzy?

It was light-headed!

78. What do sea creatures fall sick with?

Eel-nesses (illnesses)!

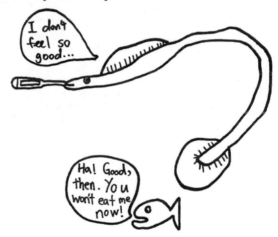

79. Why can't the pencils move?

They are stationary (stationery)!

80. Why did the cat loiter around the crime scene?

Something smelled fishy.

81. Which bird is the most terrifying?

A scare-crow!

82. Which tourist attraction does a cow like to visit?

A moo-seum (museum)!

83. What do you get when a dog eats a flower?

A collie-flower (cauliflower)!

84. Someone broke into a home and took nothing but burgers. Why was that so?

It was a burger-ry (burglary)!

85. Why did the man take part in the marathon even though he had a cold?

He had a runny nose!

86. What schedule do herbs follow?

A thyme-table (timetable)!

87. Why wasn't the fisherman popular?

His job made him selfish (sell fish)!

Did you know... the biggest fish caught was a great white shark in Australia that weighed 1208 kilograms? That is about the weight of a car!

We weigh the same!

88. Why did the horse go to the hairdresser?

It wanted to get a pony-tail!

89. What type of cup is the loudest?

A hic-cup!

90. Why did the detective pull a blanket over himself?

He wanted to go under-cover!

91. Why did the barber win the race?

He knew how to take a short-cut!

92. Why did the lady bring the bucket to the doctor's?

The bucket was a little pale (pail).

93. What vehicle has big wheels, sharp teeth and a pair of horns?

A monster truck!

Growl!~

94. What type of musical intruments live in our head?

Ear-drums!

95. Why is the Mathematics teacher so wise?

She gives plenty of add-vice (advice)!

96. Why did the farmer start to lose his voice when he walked past the stable?

He became a little hoarse (horse)!

97. What does an Eskimo use to stick things together?

An i-glue (igloo)!

98. What do you call a musical put up by cats?

A purr-formance (performance)!

99. Which animal is always ready for a holiday?

An elephant! Because it always carries its trunk with it!

Trunk

100. Why are the housefly and the tortoise good friends?

They both carry their homes with them!

101. Why did the T-rex visit the doctor?

It had a dino-sore (dinosaur)!

102. Which vegetable is the kindest?

The care-rot (carrot)!

103. Why did the lady hang bells on her ears?

She wanted to have ear-rings!

104. Why did the gardener put on green gloves?

He wanted to have green fingers!

105. Which drink makes you fall sick?

Cough-fee (coffee)!

106. Which insect is the strongest?

A ter-might (termite)!

107. What animal do you get when a pig falls into a bush?

A hedge-hog!

108. Which room is too small to fit any furniture in?

A mush-room!

109. What smells the most on our face?

Our nose!

110. What fruit do you get when a key goes down a slide?

A key-whee (kiwi)! Because the key goes, "Wheee!" down the slide!

111. Why was the boulder so unfeeling?

It had a heart of stone!

112. What is a scarecrow's favourite fruit?

The straw-berry!

create your own drawing!

113. Why did the people stand outside in the rain for a meeting?

They were trying to brain-storm ideas!

114. Why was the ballerina so alert?

She was always on her toes!

115. Why did the boy walk slowly across the beach?

He did not want to fall into quick-sand!

116. What animal can you use to hit a ball?

A bat!

117. Which of the four seasons has the most awards?

Win-ter!

118. Why did the lady step on soybeans?

She wanted to make toe-fu (tofu)!

119. Why did the book have a sharp sense of hearing?

It had a dog ear!

120. Why does the dog like to live in the wrestling ring?

It is a Boxer!

121. What is a fish's favourite breakfast?

Sea-real (cereal)!

122. Which dinosaur can fly and is scary?

A terror-dactyl (pterodactyl)!

123. Which number has a bad memory?

The number '4' because it often four-gets (forgets)!

124. Why did the worm sleep in?

It did not want to get eaten by the early bird!

125. Why couldn't the shark stop laughing?

It had just eaten a clownfish!

126. What size of clothes does Superman wear?

He wears the size 'small' because there is the letter 'S' on his top!

127. What do you get when you drop a cup of water?

A water-fall!

128. Why did the skeleton feel cold during story time?

He heard a bone-chilling story!

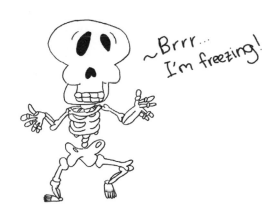

129. Why did the kettle moo?

**It thought it was a member of
the cattle family!**

130. What did the car owner say to the wheel that
was too worn out?

It's time to re-tire!

131. Why was the jack-o'-lantern scared of
the dark?

It had no guts!

132. Which of our body parts are the most reliable?

Our fingers! Because they can be counted on!

133. What did the bear use to help its plants to grow well?

Fur-tiliser (fertiliser)!

134. Why was the king in pain?

He was aching (a king)!

135. Which seafood does a bodybuilder eat to get stronger?

Mussels (muscles)!

66 **Did you know...**

mussels have threads called 'beards' that help them hold onto rocks? That way, the mussels will not be washed away easily by waves! 99

→Mussel

→Beard

136. Which is older, a raisin or a grape? Why?

A raisin is older than a grape because a raisin has more wrinkles!

137. Why didn't the archer have many friends?

He was too arrow-gant (arrogant)!

138. How can you tell that the wedding cake was sad?

It was in tears (tiers)!

139. Which vehicle is sleepy all the time?

The bull-dozer!

140. How can you make a monkey rich?

By taking the letter 'k' away from it!

141. Why are the numbers 1, 3, and 5 strange?

They are odd numbers!

142. Why did the gardener hang a painting of a nut on the wall?

He wanted to grow a wall-nut (walnut) tree!

143. What do you call an angry Santa Claus?

Santa Cross!

144. What is a giraffe's favourite drink?

Neck-tar (nectar)!

145. Why did the scientist throw a brick through a window?

He wanted to make a break-through in his discovery!

146. How can a snake become a pop star?

By rapping! Because snakes are rap-tiles (reptiles)!

147. What type of hair does a moose have on its face?

A moose-tache (moustache)!

148. What type of footwear do ninjas wear?

They wear sneakers so they can sneak around!

149. How can we turn a diary into milk?

By switching the letters 'i' and 'a'!

150. What pet can you drive around?

A car-pet!

The End!

GET FREE COLOURING PAGES!

Building a relationship with our readers is the most rewarding thing about writing. We occasionally send emails about new releases, special offers, and other news related to our family!

If you sign up for our no-spam newsletter at https://geni.us/OP1zwZ, we will send you free colouring pages made up of the illustrations from this book!

Here is the QR code to sign up:

Interested in purchasing more copies or placing a bulk order?

Scan the QR code below to visit our Singapore website at https://geni.us/orderaaronsbook for more info:

Enjoyed this book?
You can make a big difference!

Reviews are the best gifts that readers (like you!) can give writers (like us!). They go a long way to help our books get discovered by others.

If this book has brought you laughter and joy, we would be so grateful if you could take a few minutes to leave a review (as short or as long as you like) on the book's Amazon page or Goodreads page. It would mean the world to us. You can jump right to the page by visiting the websites below or scanning the QR codes.

Amazon page:
https://geni.us/f2ZGJ

QR code:

Goodreads page:
https://geni.us/LQcBWN1

QR code:

Thank you so much!
Keep in contact with us through:
Our **website** at monster-thinkery.myshopify.com
Instagram at @monsterthinkery
Facebook at Monster Thinkery
TikTok at @monsterthinkery and
our **email** at lia@monsterthinkery.com

~WOOF! GIMME A HIGH FIVE!

ABOUT THE AUTHORS

Lia Leow is a mother of three resilient little ones—a cancer survivor (Aaron), a burn survivor (Robin) and a Kawasaki disease survivor (Alexa). She has written more than 80 English and Science educational books. Lia also co-founded the publishing house, Monster Thinkery, with her children to inspire young thinkers through fun stories.

Aaron Tay is a 9-year-old cancer survivor. He is now working hard to tick items off his bucket list. The first item on his list is to be a Pokémon trainer. The second is to publish books written by children for other children. He hopes to raise awareness about pediatric cancer and inspire others to live, love and laugh every day.

ABOUT THE ILLUSTRATOR

Robin Tay is a 7-year-old burn survivor. He spends most of his time drawing—monsters, vehicles, candies—if you can name it, he can draw it! When Robin is not drawing, he is busy dismantling things and figuring out how they work. Whenever Robin feels like taking something apart, his family comes up with a new book idea for him to illustrate!

ABOUT THE CHEERLEADER

Alexa Tay is a 3-year-old Kawasaki disease survivor. She was born at the start of the pandemic while her oldest brother was undergoing chemotherapy. Although Alexa has to spend most of her time indoors because of lockdowns, she is full of joy and curiosity. Alexa may be too young to write or illustrate, but she cheers the team on by showering them with cuddles and kisses!

ALSO BY LIA LEOW, AARON TAY AND ROBIN TAY

Alexa wants you to get our latest book!

Keep a look out for it on our social media!

If you have any ideas or a book you would like to see come to life, feel free to contact us!

DEDICATION

To Ian, a supportive husband, an amazing daddy and our pillar of strength. And to our entire village who has been standing by our side through all these years, thank you for holding our hands and lifting us up in moments of darkness.

ACKNOWLEDGEMENTS

We would like to thank my brother, Ash Leow, for his invaluable help with the business side of publishing this book and for believing in this project.

Our family is also so thankful to Melissa Lee for helping us to design the amazing cover and format the book.

To Melanie Sim and Adrian Lee, thank you for helping us to edit and proofread the book.

Last but not least, we wish to thank Children Cancer Foundation (CCF) for their unwavering support.

Without them, this book would not have been possible. Thank you all for helping Aaron and Robin to fulfill their dreams.

COPYRIGHT

A Monster Thinkery book.
First published in Singapore in 2022 by Monster Thinkery
Book first published in 2022 by Monster Thinkery
Copyright © Monster Thinkery